I'm a Pterodactyl

CHERRY LAKE PRESS

Published in the United States of America by Cherry Lake Publishing
Ann Arbor, Michigan
www.cherrylakepublishing.com

Reading Adviser: Marla Conn, MS, Ed., Literacy specialist, Read-Ability, Inc.
Content Adviser: Kierstin Rosenbach, Ph.D. Candidate, Vertebrate Paleontology, University of Michigan
Book Designer: Jennifer Wahi
Illustrator: Jeff Bane

Photo Credits: © Artem Avetisyan/Shutterstock.com, 5; © Independent birds/Shutterstock.com, 7; © Photomontage/Shutterstock.com, 9; © Keni/Shutterstock.com, 11; © Catmando/Shutterstock.com, 13, 23; © YuRi Photolife/Shutterstock.com, 15; © British Library, 063983, 17; © Damsea/Shutterstock.com, 19; © MZPHOTO.CZ/Shutterstock.com, 21; Cover, 2-3, 6, 20, 22, 24, Jeff Bane

Library of Congress Cataloging-in-Publication Data

Names: Nelson, Jake, author. | Bane, Jeff, 1957- illustrator.
Title: I'm a pterodactyl / Jake Nelson; illustrator, Jeff Bane.
Description: Ann Arbor, Michigan: Cherry Lake Publishing, [2021] | Series: My dinosaur adventure | Includes index. | Audience: Grades K-1
Identifiers: LCCN 2020002491 (print) | LCCN 2020002492 (ebook) | ISBN 9781534168497 (hardcover) | ISBN 9781534170179 (paperback) | ISBN 9781534172012 (pdf) | ISBN 9781534173859 (ebook)
Subjects: LCSH: Pterodactyls--Juvenile literature.
Classification: LCC QE862.P7 N45 2021 (print) | LCC QE862.P7 (ebook) | DDC 567.918--dc23
LC record available at https://lccn.loc.gov/2020002491
LC ebook record available at https://lccn.loc.gov/2020002492

Printed in the United States of America
Corporate Graphics

table of contents

About the author: Jake Nelson was born and raised in Minnesota, where he enjoys everything from watching the Twins at Target Field to strolling along the shore of Lake Superior. He writes books, blogs, and content for the web.

About the illustrator: Jeff Bane and his two business partners own a studio along the American River in Folsom, California, home of the 1849 Gold Rush. When Jeff's not sketching or illustrating for clients, he's either swimming or kayaking in the river to relax.

I am a Pterodactyl.
And guess what? I can fly!

I have two wings, like a bird.

But I do not have feathers.

I am not a bird.

I am a **reptile**.

I am not very large.

My wings are only 3 feet (1 meter) long.

I lived 150 million years ago, in the **Mesozoic era**.

My name means "winged finger."

My wings are **elongated** fingers.

My wings help me catch my food.

I'm a **carnivore**.

Sometimes my **prey** is insects.

But most of the time, I like eating fish.

Can you name
an animal
with a long beak?

I have a long beak.

I use it to catch fish.

What makes you unique?

I am proud to rule the sky.

There is no creature like me.

glossary & index

glossary

carnivore (KAHR-nuh-vor) a creature that only eats other living things, like animals or bugs

elongated (ih-LAWNG-gate-id) stretched out to become longer than usual

Mesozoic era (mez-uh-ZOH-ik ER-uh) the period of time when dinosaurs lived on Earth, between 245 million and 66 million years ago

prey (PRAY) a creature that is hunted by another creature

reptile (REP-tye-uhl) a kind of animal with scaly skin, usually with a tail; lizards and snakes are reptiles

index